Sarah Saves the Day

An Almost Forgotten Story from the American Revolutionary War with Educational Activities

Ellen Chervenick

Ellen Chervenick
www.SarahBradleeFultonMuseum.com
www.Facebook.com/Sarah-Saves-the-Day-An-Almost-Forgotten-Story

Cover art by Ellen Chervenick

Cover design by BookCoverDesigns.net

Author portrait by Savannah Chervenick

Photographs on pages 2 and 8 by Ellen Chervenick

Illustrations on pages 5, 13, 26, 39, and 43 by Ellen Chervenick

Photo on page 10 used with permission by Lauren Hands

Photograph on page 15, *The Bradlee House*, 1898, Boston Public Library, accessed August 28, 2020, https://www.flickr.com/photos/boston_public_library/2885420978.

Illustration on page 16, *The Bloody Massacre*, 1770, Boston Athenaeum, accessed August 28, 2020, https://www.bostonathenaeum.org/about/publications/selections-acquired-tastes/bloody-massacre

The map on page 36, *Siege of Boston* 1775-76, was accessed August 28, 2020, https://www.battlefields.org/learn/maps/siege-boston

Proofreading by Piney Woods Editorial Services

Book Layout © 2017 BookDesignTemplates.com
Formatting by DanelleYoung.com

Sarah Saves the Day/ Ellen Chervenick. – 1st ed.
Library of Congress Control Number: 2020921429
Paperback ISBN: 978-0-578-74273-1
eBook ISBN: 978-0-578-77767-2

To Amanda, Savannah, Leland, Alex, and Éowyn

Well-behaved women seldom make history.
—Laurel Thatcher Ulrich

AUTHOR'S NOTE

This is a work of historical fiction based on a true story. Much of the conversation contained in this book is fictional, but it is based on dialogue that did take place, and wherever possible, incorporates actual phrases used by the speaker.

PREFACE

My maternal grandmother, Madeleine Rindge Hands, often told me these true stories about my great-great-great-great-great-grandmother, Sarah Bradlee Fulton. I hope that by writing this book that Sarah's story will not be forgotten and that her important role in the American Revolution will not be lost.

I created this book's activities for fifth graders studying U.S. History; however, all ages can participate. They include embroidery, drinking tea, singing, reading a map, and baking. Other sensory experiences could incorporate sewing, crafts, chores (like churning butter), looking at picture books, and dancing colonial-style.

Studies have shown that students of history learn and retain more information when presented with correlating activities that involve as many of the senses as possible. I researched this concept, which is called Schema Theory (the idea that words do not have meaning unless the person reading them has a background knowledge or mental scaffolding in the brain; the more sensory input, the more scaffolding in the brain).

My ESL (English as a Second Language) students were the subjects of my research. I taught half of the students a history lesson about Abraham Lincoln with no sensory input—just reading the information. The other half read the same lesson, but with sensory input, like slides, music, costumes, and food from that period. The students who experienced sensory input scored significantly higher on a test about Lincoln.

Contents

Chapter 1

THE MYSTERY OF THE LAFAYETTE PIN

Altadena, California, and Crestwood, New York, 1964

My story begins with a memory from my childhood. I am ten years old, and it's a sunny spring day in Altadena, California. My mom picks me up from school and tells me, "We need to go to the bank today. There's something important that we need to do."

"What is it?" I ask.

"I'll tell you when we get to the safe-deposit box."

We quietly walk into the solemn atmosphere of the old bank, where my mom signs a paper, and a bank teller leads us behind giant metal doors to a row of safe-deposit boxes. We sit down in a private cubicle, and my mom brings out a small, white box from her purse. I recognize my grandmother's handwriting and the words "Lafayette pin" written on it. My mother opens the box and shows me a tiny piece of jewelry. "This is the Lafayette pin," Mom says in hushed tones, as she holds it gently in her hands.

"Grandma gave this to me the last time we visited her in New York. Ellen, did you know that General Lafayette came over from France to help the Americans win the Revolutionary War in the 1700s?"

I shake my head. "No."

Mom continues. "When he came back to visit America in 1824, he gave this to your great-great-great-great-great-grandmother, Sarah Bradlee Fulton. It was a special gift to thank her for the brave things she did to help the Americans win independence from the British. This pin has been passed down through all the generations of oldest daughters, starting with Sarah's oldest daughter, Sarah Lloyd. I am Grandma's oldest daughter, and you are my oldest girl. So, you will inherit this pin from me in the future. I'm putting it into this safe-deposit box, so it won't get lost or stolen. We need to keep it secure."

I smile at my mom, curious about this brave, female ancestor.

"I promise to take good care of it when I am older, Mom."

She hands me the pin, and I gently hold it in the palm of my hand. It is smaller than a dime. Pearls surround a red garnet in a gold setting.

GEN. LA-FAYETTE

Lafayette's pin and the etching from 1824 are kept together.

"What is the story behind this pin?" I ask. "Do you know what brave things Sarah did in the Revolutionary War to earn a gift like this?"

"I don't know anything more about her story. But I do know that it wasn't just men who played important roles in American history. Women played important roles too, but sadly, many stories about women in history have been lost or forgotten. Grandma might know more about Sarah's story. Let's ask her about it when we visit this summer."

Mom and I land in New York on June 14, 1964. Grandpa and Grandma meet us at the airport. I love them both so much, and I run to hug them. I feel how much they love me and Mom. Then, we climb into their Oldsmobile car, and Grandpa drives us north, heading toward their home in Crestwood.

"We'll be driving past the fairgrounds in a minute," he says. "If you look to your left, you can see the giant, metal sculpture of the Earth at the entrance. It's the symbol of the World's Fair, whose theme is 'peace through understanding.'"

I press my face against the window to see the sculpture. Mom and I will be going to the fair in a few days with my Aunt Muriel and cousins, Linda and Herb. I'm looking forward to going to the World's Fair, but I want to ask my grandparents about our family history sometime before that.

"Grandpa, Mom was telling me that we have a woman on Grandma's side who played an important role in the American Revolution. Do you know if we have women like that on your side, too?

"Well, yes, we do! My parents both were doctors, and my mother was one of the first female doctors in Boston in the 1800s."

"That's quite an accomplishment for your mother, Grandpa! And Grandma, didn't you graduate from Smith College in the early 1900's when it was unusual for women to go to College?"

"Yes, Ellen, and I majored in Botany."

When we get to their house in Crestwood, I hear the familiar sound of the car wheels crunching on the gravel driveway.

I run into the kitchen to hug Savannah, my grandparents' cook, who is getting the dinner ready for us. It smells delicious, and Savannah smells good too—like pie crust. I love her, and she loves me like I am her adopted granddaughter.

We sit down to a scrumptious dinner, followed by lemon meringue pie, Savannah's specialty. I wait until after dinner to ask Grandma about Sarah.

"Grandma, will you please tell me the story of Sarah Bradlee Fulton? What did she do to get a pin from General Lafayette?"

"Ellen, I was wondering about that, too, and I found an article the other day at the library about Sarah's life, written by another descendant of hers—Helen Tilden Wild."

Grandma reaches behind her and picks up some papers from the chiffonier chest of drawers. "It's hot tonight, so let's go sit down outside on the screened back porch, and I will tell you all about this amazing story."

As Mom, Grandpa, and I get settled into the comfortable patio chairs, Grandma begins. "I took some notes on the article I read. It was written in 1898. Sarah Bradlee was the fifth child of Samuel and Mary Bradlee. She was born on December 24, 1740, in Dorchester, Massachusetts."

"So, she was a Christmas baby, just like me!"

"Yes, she was, dear. It must have been cold and snowy on the night she was born . . ."

Sarah's Home

A GIRL'S LIFE IN THE MASSACHUSETTS COLONY

Boston, Massachusetts, 1750–1762

One warm, spring morning in the Massachusetts colony, Sarah poured cold water from a wooden bucket along the row of vegetables, then walked back to the water pump to fill the bucket again so she could water the next row in the garden. At ten-years-old, she had many chores left to do before she could go explore the marshes along the Mystic River. She had to feed hay to the cows, oxen, and horses, and collect eggs from the chickens. Then she had to collect firewood and light it in the fireplace to heat up the large metal kettle that was placed over the fireplace for cooking. She cooked oatmeal in the kettle and served it to her family with maple syrup. After breakfast, she had to heat up water in the kettle to wash the dishes. She also had to help tidy up the house with her mother and sisters before she left. Later, she would churn the butter and work on her sampler.

Did you know that girls in colonial times worked on samplers—decorative needlework which taught them how to sew? They were responsible for sewing clothes for the family as soon as they could master their samplers.

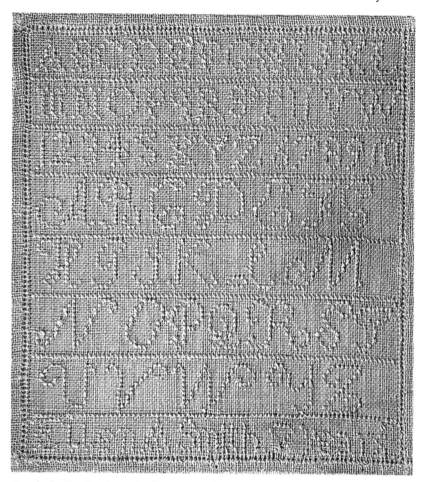

Sampler by Ellen Antoinette Smith, age seven. She was born on July 29, 1824, in Lexington, MA.

ACTIVITY ~ EMBROIDERY

LEARN SOME EASY EMBROIDERY STITCHES AND PRACTICE ON A PIECE OF FABRIC USING A SMALL EMBROIDERY HOOP. THEN, DRAW A DESIGN (LIKE YOUR INITIALS OR A SIMPLE FLOWER) WITH A PENCIL ON A SHIRT, BANDANA, OR DISH TOWEL. EMBROIDER USING THE PENCIL LINES AS A GUIDE.

Happy to be finished with her morning chores, Sarah sprinted across to the marsh to find her favorite tree. She peered down inside the knothole. There was a piece of paper. A note from John!

John Fulton and his parents, Samuel and Elizabeth, were neighbors of the Bradlee family. John didn't seem to mind that Sarah was a tomboy. She loved climbing trees and pretending to solve mysteries. She was fearless and bold.

"Finally, I have a friend who understands me," she said softly to herself.

She opened the note, and it said, "Let's go fishing at the river next Saturday. Bring your brother, Nathaniel."

Sarah tucked the note into her pocket and smiled.

John and Sarah kept leaving notes for each other in the hollow of the tree for the next ten years. They were fellow adventurers and best friends, so it was no surprise when, one freezing day in March 1762, Sarah reached into the knothole and pulled out a message which read, "Sarah, will you marry me?"

Did you know that most girls at that time got married around the age of twenty or they began to be considered too old?

Sarah ran home and asked her parents' permission.

"Why can't John ask us himself?" her father asked.

"He's shy about things like this," Sarah answered. "But on the positive side, he has been successful as a rum distiller and bookkeeper recently, so he can afford to get married now."

Her mom said, "Your father and I will talk about it and then give you our answer."

Later that night, Sarah ran out to the tree and left a one-word message for John—yes!

Sarah and John were married in her parents' home by a Presbyterian minister named Reverend John Moorhead. Sarah looked stunning in her forest-green brocade dress with a high waistline, which she had made herself. A salmon-colored ruffle peeked over the neck-line. On July 25, 1762, Sarah Bradlee became Mrs. Sarah Bradlee Fulton.

Did you know that weddings were commonly held at the bride's parents' home? They were not usually held at a church with bridesmaids and groomsmen like today. Women in colonial times were not married in white dresses, either. Brides wore many colors for their wedding. Poor brides often wore black. Brides with more money wore a dress of colorful, lush fabric. At the time, a white wedding dress was considered impractical because the bride would often wear her wedding dress for other dress-up occasions. White fabric showed the dirt too much. Queen Victoria wore a white dress for her wedding in 1840. She started the trend that would continue to the present day.

Sarah Bradlee Fulton's wedding dress modeled by my cousin, Lauren Hands.

Chapter 3

SONS AND DAUGHTERS OF LIBERTY AND THE BOSTON MASSACRE

Boston, 1765-March 5,1770

Not long after John and Sarah got married, the political times began to change in the colonies. The British King George III imposed oppressive taxes on imported fabric, tea, and other items that the colonists valued highly. The Sugar Act charged tax on sugar and molasses (used for making rum), and the Stamp Act charged taxes on newspapers and other important papers. The Townsend Act charged tax on British imports like tea, glass, and paint. Reverend Moorehead invited Sarah and John to a protest meeting at the Presbyterian church to discuss what could be done about the problem of the ridiculous British taxes. When they arrived, the group was already angry.

"Unfair taxes!" called one man.

"No taxation without representation!" yelled others.

Reverend Moorehead called for the meeting to come to order. "Yes, we are all in agreement that these taxes are unfair, and even worse, we have no vote in England about them. However, we are intelligent people. Let's take the time to think about what we can do about it."

After much discussion, everyone agreed that they would not buy any British imports. So, this included not buying the beautiful, expensive fabric that they used to make their clothes, especially dresses (like Sarah's wedding dress). Instead, they would spin their own thread and weave their own fabric. They called it "homespun."

Sarah and John decided then and there that they would go along with this protest. After the meeting, Sarah became involved in "spinning bees" to produce the homespun fabric. She and her friends spun hemp, linen, flax, wool, and other materials into yarn to make cloth. As if women didn't have enough chores to do already!

Spinning Wheel

They also boycotted (refused to buy) imported tea from Britain. At that time, tea drinking was extremely popular with the colonists; it was one of the most important traditions of their day. Instead, they drank "Liberty Tea." It was the patriotic thing to do. Liberty Tea was made from substitute ingredients like chamomile, mint leaves, thyme, roses, violets, and sliced fruits such as strawberries and apples.

ACTIVITY ~ LIBERTY TEA

MAKE YOUR OWN LIBERTY TEA USING ONE OF THE INGREDIENTS ABOVE. BUY SOME CHAMOMILE TEA, MINT TEA OR ANOTHER HERBAL TEA AT YOUR LOCAL STORE. IF YOU WANT TO TRY SOME OF THE LEAVES, FLOWERS OR FRUITS, ADD A TABLESPOON TO YOUR TEACUP, BOIL WATER, AND CAREFULLY POUR IT OVER YOUR INGREDIENT. WAIT FIVE MINUTES AND THEN DRINK THE TEA. YOU WILL SEE WHY IT WAS A SACRIFICE TO DRINK LIBERTY TEA!

Did you know that this organized boycott of imported cloth and tea from England was the very first nonviolent protest in American history—and it was led and carried out by women?

Sarah and many other women involved in the protest were members of the Daughters of Liberty, a radical group of strong-willed women who wanted freedom from England. Sarah was not only a member of this group, but she was also a leader. Some other members of the Daughters of Liberty were Abigail Adams (wife of John Adams), Martha Washington (wife of George Washington), Sarah Franklin Bache (daughter of diplomat Benjamin Franklin), and Elizabeth Nichols Dyar (Sarah Fulton's friend and Patriot in Boston).

John joined the Sons of Liberty. They often met at the Green Dragon, a pub in Boston. Some of the members of the Sons of Liberty were Samuel Adams and his second cousin, John Adams, Paul Revere, Benedict Arnold, John Hancock, and Patrick Henry. These men and women would go on to play important roles in the American Revolution and the new government.

Sarah's brother Nathaniel Bradlee, a carpenter and fisherman, was also part of the Sons of Liberty and well known as a Patriot. He and his wife Anne lived on the corner of Hollis and Tremont streets in Boston.

The Bradlee Home in Boston

Nathaniel started a tradition of inviting other Patriots over for codfish dinners at his house every Saturday night. During dinner, these large groups of famous Patriots were usually having heated discussions about current political events. Sarah and John often attended with their growing family. Eventually, they would have ten children!

1) Sarah Lloyd born on May 20, 1764

2) John Andrews born on December 15, 1765

3) Ann Wier born on December 23, 1767

4) Mary born on February 10, 1770 (Died of smallpox in 1775)

5) Lydia born on April 22, 1772

6) Frances Burns born on August 13 (?), 1774

7) Mary #2, born on February 5, 1777

8) Samuel Bradlee born on March 3, 1779

9) Lucretia Butler born on January 10, 1782

10) Elizabeth Scott born on June 5, 1784

One cold morning, in March 1770, Sarah and her children (Sarah Lloyd, John, Ann, and baby Mary) were on their way to visit Nathaniel and Anne when a young man approached them and handed her a flyer. It was an illustration by Paul Revere.

Paul Revere's print of British soldiers firing on townspeople

As she looked at it, Sarah's face turned bright red with anger. "Oh, my God. This is just too much!"

"What is it, Mama?" asked her six-year-old daughter, Sarah Lloyd.

"A terrible thing happened a couple of weeks ago," Sarah said, as she held up the picture for her daughter to see. "You know that the British soldiers have been causing trouble in Boston since they got here in 1768, right? They arrived when you were four, dear. Well, they just keep causing problems for us and won't stop! Last night there was a British soldier standing outside of the Old State House. He was trying to keep the peace amidst a lot of rising tension and anger between the colonists and the British. The Patriots began calling the soldier some names because they were so furious about how badly the British have treated us. Some other British soldiers saw this happening and tried to help and defend him. However, this caused the Patriots to be scared and yell more. So, then the Patriots started throwing snowballs, rocks, and sticks at the British soldiers."

Sarah pointed to the picture. "The British officers fired rifles into the crowd without orders, instantly killing three Patriots (a black sailor named Crispus Attucks, a rope maker, Samuel Gray, and a mariner named James Caldwell). They wounded eight other people, and now two of them have died."

Sarah started crying. Then she crumpled the drawing and pulled her children close. "This is why we must fight for our freedom. Now with these vicious shootings, the British have gone too far. There's no going back now!"

Chapter 4

THE LAST STRAW

Boston, November 29, 1773

*T*he people of Boston continued to have more of the same kinds of trouble with the British over the next three years. It escalated and became worse and worse, but the most distressing problem had to do with the unfair taxes charged on tea.

One chilly but sunny morning, Sarah was hanging up laundry in the backyard when her brother Nathaniel rushed up.

"Sarah, a ship called the *Dartmouth* just docked at Griffin's Wharf, and two more ships will be docking soon. It must be the East India Company! Those three ships are loaded with 342 chests of that darn Bohea (pronounced *boh-hee*). That tea is disgusting! And they have the nerve to charge us more taxes on tea that doesn't even taste good. This is the last straw!"

"Yes, I just heard the news, and our neighbor says there will be a meeting tonight at the Old South Meeting House. We are going! How about you, Nathaniel?"

"We will meet you there in the front row on the right side."

At the meeting that night, the people petitioned Governor Hutchinson to send the ships back to England because they didn't want the tea to be unloaded. If the tea was unloaded, they would be forced to pay a tax on it. But there was a problem. Governor

Hutchinson denied the petition, and, to make matters worse, the law required that a ship's cargo be unloaded within twenty days of its arrival in the harbor.

Twenty days later, on December 16, 1773, the problem still had not been resolved, and Governor Hutchison still said, "No," to the petition to send the ships back. In the meantime, the Sons of Liberty were thinking of dumping all 342 chests of tea into the harbor! Sarah had thought of a way to disguise the Patriot men as Mohawk Indians as they dumped the tea because their identities had to be hidden. They would be risking their lives if they were recognized while they were carrying out this radical act.

You may be wondering why they thought it was a good idea to dress as Indians and wear warpaint. Today, this idea would be considered to be an insult to Native Americans and would be politically incorrect. However, at that time, they knew that the British wouldn't actually believe that they were Indians; it was a symbolic way of identifying themselves as Americans along with the Native Americans in a positive sense. They were making a statement that they were no longer British but independent Americans.

Old South Meeting House
Boston, 10:00 am, December 16, 1773

That morning, Sarah and her family gathered with five thousand angry Boston citizens at the old church. More than a third of Boston's whole population crowded into the church, filling up every pew, gallery, and aisle. The captain of the *Dartmouth* was there. He told the crowd that he couldn't leave the harbor unless he unloaded the tea.

"We will help you unload it! Ha! Let's dump the tea into the harbor!" yelled one furious Patriot in the front row.

"Aye!" shouted the people.

Then the captain spoke up. "I am a Quaker, so because of my pacifist religion, I don't want to be involved in any violence. The other two captains are Quakers also. We will not fight back, but this must be a peaceful takeover of our ships."

"Aye, aye, Captain!"

The Patriots rushed out of the meeting and began shouting.

"On to Griffin's Wharf!"

Sarah's disguising idea had become popular, and many of the Patriots had already planned their Mohawk Indian outfits. Nathaniel Bradlee and his family and friends were ready to put their costumes and war paint on.

Later that night, a full moon rose over Boston. Inside Nathaniel and Anne's house, the kitchen was quickly filling up with men carrying hatchets and axes.

Sarah noticed the weapons. "Hey, you boys know that you're not supposed to be violent, right?"

"Yes, Sarah. It's only for whacking the boxes of tea open!"

"Well, alright, then. Let's get your war paint on."

Sarah and Anne began hurriedly smearing black soot and red paint on the men's faces. Sarah put the final touches of paint on John's face. Her brothers Nathaniel, David, Thomas, and Josiah were also participating. As soon as their faces were painted, some of the men started walking toward the door, but Sarah ordered, "Hey, not so fast, Mohawks. Don't forget to put those old blankets over your shoulders. There's a whole pile of 'em over there, by the door."

"Yes, ma'am," they replied.

All these men knew they were about to participate in an event that could lead to being jailed or killed by the British. What they did not know was that the actions they were about to carry out would change American history forever.

Chapter 5

THE MOTHER OF THE BOSTON TEA PARTY

Boston, December 16, 1773

As the town clock struck 7:00 pm, Sarah poked her head out the door and peered down the street. She looked at her husband and whispered, "Okay, go!"

John, disguised as a Mohawk Indian, crept out into the night. The men left one by one every thirty seconds so as not to draw attention to the Bradlee house. When the last man had left, Anne opened the door again. "Go on and follow the men if you want, Sarah. I'll watch the children. I know you don't want to miss out on any of the adventure."

Sarah pulled a shawl around her shoulders.

"Thank you, Anne!"

It had rained earlier that day, but it was clear now. The night air was fresh as she hurried down the shiny cobblestone street in the moonlight. Walking down Cow Lane, Sarah was surprised to see a massive crowd standing on the shore at Griffin's Wharf. She hid next to a brick building and peered around the corner to watch the action. All attention was on the tea ships—the *Dartmouth*, the *Eleanor*, and the brig *Beaver*.

When the "Mohawk Indians" reached the three ships, they divided into three groups and boarded each of the vessels. Sarah heard their loud whoops as each party of men nonviolently forced the customs officers off the ships and onto the shore. As promised in the meeting, the officers and captains of these ships cooperated and didn't fight back.

The boats creaked as the Patriots hauled the heavy tea chests up from the hold and broke them open with their axes. They shoveled the tea over the edge of the ship and hoisted the chests over the railing after it. British naval ships were present in the harbor, just a few hundred yards out past the tea ships. Yet, they did not intervene. They were afraid that if they did, it would get violent like the Boston Massacre.

On Griffin's Wharf, the crowd became even larger, but they remained unusually silent. Sarah and the others could only hear the whack of the axes breaking the chests of tea. Sarah could feel the solemn moment. *This is a very important moment; I am witnessing history!*

Sarah watched the great piles of tea leaves floating on the water in the moonlight, drifting to shore by the shifting tide. Along the beach, scavengers started to scoop up handfuls of tea into their pockets. A Patriot barked orders to a group of young boys on the shore.

"Hey, you boys, destroy that tea!"

All the tea had to be destroyed so that no one could profit from it. The boys quickly went into action along the murky mudflats. Barelegged and barefoot, they stomped the tea into the mud and saltwater.

"Boston Harbor a teapot tonight!" they cheered.

Did you know that George Washington, Benjamin Franklin, and some other Patriots disapproved of the Boston Tea Party? They viewed it as unnecessary vandalism. However, most of the Patriots were completely "on board" (ha) with the Boston Tea Party! The following song became popular, and people sang it in the streets:

"Rally Mohawks! bring out your axes,
And tell King George we'll pay no taxes
On his foreign tea;
His threats are vain, and vain to think
To force our girls and wives to drink
His vile Bohea!"

ACTIVITY ~ SING

SING THE ABOVE SONG AND MAKE UP YOUR OWN MELODY OR SIMPLY READ IT. ANOTHER MORE CURRENT SONG THAT COULD BE PLAYED AND LEARNED BY STUDENTS IS "THE BOSTON TEA PARTY SONG" BY JAM CAMPUS (A PARODY OF "HAPPY" BY PHARRELL WILLIAMS) ON YOUTUBE.

Seeing that the men's work was almost done, Sarah turned and bolted back up the street into the night. When she arrived home, she found Anne heating water in the big copper boiler to clean the war paint off the men's faces.

"The men will be returning soon!" she said breathlessly.

As the town clock struck ten o'clock, the men began to rush in. The two women scrubbed the men's faces as fast as possible. As they finished, they heard bushes rustling outside the window. Sarah silently gestured for the men to go upstairs. Sarah and Anne acted like they were busy in the kitchen. Out of the corner of her eye, Sarah saw a British soldier spying on them through the window. But he would only see two calm, unruffled women cooking something in a big copper boiler—nothing unusual here—just two women doing their regular chores. Sarah had saved the day!

A British soldier spies on Sarah and Anne.

Did you know that this act of defiance against the most powerful nation in the world would later be known as the Boston Tea Party? Sarah was called the "Mother of the Boston Tea Party," but most people these days have never heard of her—an example of how women's important roles in history are often forgotten and their stories lost.

"Shoot Away!"

Medford, Massachusetts, 1775

hen the news of the Patriots dumping the tea into the harbor reached the British King George, he was furious and wanted revenge! The British severely punished the colonists for their act of rebellion. King George and the British government passed the Intolerable Acts, which shut down Boston Harbor for business until the Colonists could pay England back for the money lost in the Tea Party. Also, British troops of soldiers were sent to control the Massachusetts Colony and to replace the Governor with a British one, General Thomas Gage. Two years after the Boston Tea Party, the Patriots fought the British at Lexington and Concord on April 19, 1775. Paul Revere had ridden past Sarah's house the night before, on April 18, yelling, "The British are coming!" This warned the townspeople of the attack that would follow the next day, so they were ready to fight back.

Because the Americans did fight back, it caused the British to retreat back to Boston and to maintain their control over the city. Within days, 20,000 Continental soldiers were rallied to surround Boston to keep the British from advancing inland from the city, in a siege that would last more than a year. The British soldiers were trapped in the city of Boston, and the Patriots left in Boston were trapped there with them. Wood and other essentials were in short supply for everyone there. However, the British had the authority to take anything they wanted, which infuriated the Patriots.

Sarah and John lived in Medford, just outside of Boston. They were safe from the siege, but they were still affected by the scarcity of supplies. One day, Sarah was at home with the children. John came running into the house, out of breath. "Sarah, I paid for a load of wood, but some redcoats stole it from me!"

Did you know that the Patriots often referred to the British soldiers as "redcoats" and "lobsterbacks" because of their red uniforms?

Sarah and John had planned to give this wood to her brother Nathaniel and other Patriots trapped in Boston. John quickly explained how he had been heading home from the harbor with their ox cart loaded with the wood. When he was almost home, some British soldiers caught up to him and aimed their rifles at him, yelling, "Stop, or we'll shoot!"

"So, I climbed down from the cart, and those lobsterbacks drove away with it, stealing our load of wood!"

Sarah immediately threw on a shawl. The soldiers couldn't be far away yet.

"I'm not afraid of them or anyone else," Sarah exclaimed, "Those nasty redcoats won't get away with this!"

She stepped out the front door and began scurrying down the hill towards the road, hollering over her shoulder to John, "I'll be back."

Sarah raced down the road toward the harbor. It was only a few minutes before she spotted the soldiers ahead. Pulling her shawl tighter, she rushed as fast as she could. When she finally caught up with them, she called out, "Hey, you there, stop now! That belongs to me!"

One of the soldiers turned and chuckled.

"Forget it, Lady!"

They just kept on going, ignoring her. Sarah dashed ahead of them and seized hold of one of the oxen by the horns.

"Whoa!"

The oxen stopped. Summoning all her strength and talking to the oxen, she turned them both around.

"Hey, Lady! What do you think you are doing?" shouted one of the soldiers.

She turned to face the Redcoats and straightened up with her hands on her hips. She bellowed in her loudest, deepest voice, "Move over, ya bloody lobsterbacks!"

Sarah leaped up into the driver's seat of the cart, grabbed her ox whip, and began swinging it at the soldiers. They backed away from her and tumbled to the ground. She took hold of the reins firmly in her hands and clucked loudly for the oxen to run.

The soldiers started to chase after her and the cart, yelling, "Stop, or we'll shoot!"

Sarah squared her shoulders, gave them the death-glare, and shouted at the top of her lungs, "Shoot away!"

Then she quickly drove her oxen away from the soldiers, toward her home. She never looked back.

The soldiers were so astonished at this spitfire woman and her audacity that they started laughing and let her go.

Sarah may have won that battle, but the war raged on. On June 17, 1775, the British attacked Breed's Hill which was later falsely named the Battle of Bunker Hill. This attack was important because they wanted to control the whole Boston area and prevent the Continental Army from taking back Boston.

The general of the Continental Army had instructed his men not to fire their guns at the British "until they saw the whites of their eyes." As a result, many British soldiers were gunned down at close range just as they reached the top of the hill. The British still managed to take the hill, but it was a bloody battle that cost many lives.

Chapter 6 - "Shoot Away!"

Sarah could hear the gunshots echoing from the hills. The Green, a park in the center of Medford, was transformed into a field hospital to tend to wounded Patriots. Sarah led a group of women to the Green, carrying bandages and medical treatments. No doctors were available, so the women did the best they could to help treat the soldiers.

One man had a bullet lodged in his cheek. None of the women wanted to remove the bullet from his face for fear that he would be permanently disfigured. Sarah decided she would do it. With a sharp knife, she carefully cut away the delicate skin around the deeply lodged bullet. The man was brave, holding still despite the agonizing pain. Finally, Sarah was successful in reaching and removing the bullet. She later found a doctor to stitch the wound.

Years later, this grateful soldier would find Sarah to thank her for saving him that day. She barely remembered him because she had taken care of so many men that day.

Did you know that anesthesia—a drug that numbs pain during surgery—had not been invented yet? It would be invented in 1848 by TG Martin in Boston, Massachusetts.

Chapter 7

THE SECRET MESSAGE

Medford, March 2, 1776

*G*eneral Washington had arrived outside of Boston last summer, in early July. He had been chosen by the Continental Congress (the beginnings of the new American government) to take command of the scruffy, dirty, undisciplined, unorganized Patriot soldiers that were laying siege to Boston. The British still controlled the city, and that was a very big problem. Everyone wondered how this American army would succeed in kicking the British out of Boston. It seemed like an impossible dream considering the bad shape the army was in and the fact that they didn't have enough weapons or gunpowder.

Sarah and John and their children had been among the residents who had greeted Washington when he first arrived. Sarah had seen by the look on Washington's face that he was appalled at the poor condition of his army.

"I feel sorry for General Washington, John," Sarah had said. "This is supposed to be his strong, new Continental Army, but Washington will really have to whip those ragamuffins into shape if they are to beat the British!"

Because of her prominent position in the Daughters of Liberty, Sarah knew all the latest news about the war. In fact, there were some Patriots staying in the Fulton's house during the siege. She had heard lots of talk about how smart General Washington was. If anyone could outsmart the enemy, it was him. He was well-versed in espionage (spying on and tricking the enemy) from his experience in the French and Indian War. The British were spying on the Americans, too. Recently, Washington had even discovered that his surgeon general, Mr. Church, was a spy for the British. Washington would be thinking of some ways to spy on and trick the British. He knew lots of good strategies, and he also trusted in God to help him.

Did you know that George Washington's first expense as general was $333.33 to build a spy ring in Boston?

Sarah had also heard rumors of Washington's plans to get more weapons for his army. Colonel Henry Knox had brought 59 cannons weighing over sixty tons from Fort Ticonderoga, New York to Cambridge, Massachusetts, where Washington was stationed. It took three months for Knox to move the large, heavy weapons by boats, horse-drawn carts, and ox-drawn sleds. He transported them in the middle of winter over bad roads, frozen rivers, and through forests and swamps. Finally, in February, Knox and the 59 cannons arrived. All of this had to remain a secret from the British.

A pounding at the door woke Sarah from her sleep. It was only 9:00 pm, but she and the family had already gone to bed. John groaned and rolled over. Quietly, Sarah lit a candle and made her way through the dark house to the front door. She peered through the peephole in the door to see who it was. There stood young Major John Brooks, who, at 24 years old, was already a doctor and a major in George Washington's Continental Army. He was highly respected and was a close friend of George Washington's.

"Major Brooks! What are you doing out at this time of night?"

He whispered, "I have an urgent request for your husband from General Washington! Please, let me in!"

"Yes, Major Brooks, please come in."

He began to wipe his boots on the mat.

Sarah stepped back as Major John Brooks finished cleaning his boots and came into the house, along with a whoosh of freezing air.

"General Washington has a top-secret message that must be delivered to General Howe tonight!" he said

"*General Howe?*" said Sarah, surprised. "The *British* commander?"

"Yes," said the major. He lowered his voice. "General Washington is going to try to secretly fortify Dorchester Heights using the weaponry that recently arrived."

Sarah's eyes widened. If the Continental Army could occupy Dorchester Heights, a hill overlooking Boston, they might be able to drive the British out of the city.

The major continued. "But there's a problem. News of our ammunition has leaked out to the British, and they are anxiously waiting to find out where our army will attack. General Washington has asked me to find a bold man who knows the way through the Mystic River Marshes to Boston. He needs to deliver a decoy message to General Howe to deceive the British. Can John do it?"

Sarah shook her head. John was very sick and "puking" continuously. "There's no way John can do this; he can't even get out of bed!"

Did you know that "puking" was the commonly used term for vomiting at that time?

Major Brooks put his hand over his face. "Oh no, this message must be delivered tonight!"

Sarah, in a heartbeat, answered, "Well, I am not a man, but I can do it!"

"Are you sure? You will be risking your life! If the British figure out you are a spy, they will have you hanged!"

"Yes, I am sure I can do this. Trust me, I know the Mystic Marshes as well as John does."

"But Sarah—"

"I have never been afraid of man or beast, Major Brooks. I can easily do this, trust me!"

"But Sarah, we don't even have a plan for how exactly you would deliver this message directly into General Howe's hands!"

Sarah paused to think and then boldly asserted, "Then I will have to make it up as I go, depending on what's going on when I get to the British camp."

"Alright, Sarah, as long as you realize the risk you will be taking."

"Yes, I know what I'm signing up for."

Major Brooks paused, then reached inside his leather pouch and handed Washington's papers to Sarah. "You must solemnly swear to tell no one about this secret mission."

"I promise that no one will learn of this secret. I swear it."

Once Major Brooks left, Sarah moved quickly.

How am I going to carry these papers as I run through the Mystic Marshes? Wait, I have an idea! She grabbed her sewing kit and used a seam ripper to cut through the stitches of her skirt hem. Next, she tucked the papers inside and sewed the documents into the hem with some whip stitches.

Eleven-year-old Sarah Lloyd appeared in the doorway, rubbing sleep from her eyes. "What are you doing, Mama?"

Sarah smoothed her skirt. "I'm going out. General Washington needs me. Help your father if he starts puking again. I will be back by daybreak!"

Chapter 8

THE MYSTIC MARSHES

Boston, 9:30 pm, March 2, 1776

S arah stepped across the threshold of her front door out into the frozen, windy night. Mounds of snow and ice surrounded her, but the night smelled so fresh that she felt energized. Even though it was almost a full moon, she could still see a multitude of twinkling stars. Gazing up, she noted where the North Star was in case she needed to get her bearings later.

She crept across the marshes, hiding behind trees to avoid being seen by the British sentries who were posted on the Charlestown Neck. The reason that Washington needed someone who could navigate the treacherous Mystic Marshes was that no Patriots could get past the heavily guarded neck of land leading over to Charlestown. The Mystic Marshes were next to the neck of land that led to the Charlestown peninsula. Sarah and John were among the few people who were tough enough to cross these marshes. She had to hold up her skirt as she slogged on through, being careful not to get the secret message sewn into her skirt hem wet. It was bitter cold, her feet felt like ice, and she started shivering. She began wondering if this really was an impossible task,

I don't even know exactly how I'm going to deliver this to General Howe in his own headquarters, behind enemy lines. If they figure out that I am a Pa-

triot spy on a deception operation trying to distract them, they will kill me by hanging! Why did I sign up for this?

No, I can't think that way. George Washington himself is depending on me. She ran in order to keep warm and kept running all the way to the waterfront. Ah, there's a rowboat! I don't know who that belongs to, but I need to borrow it.

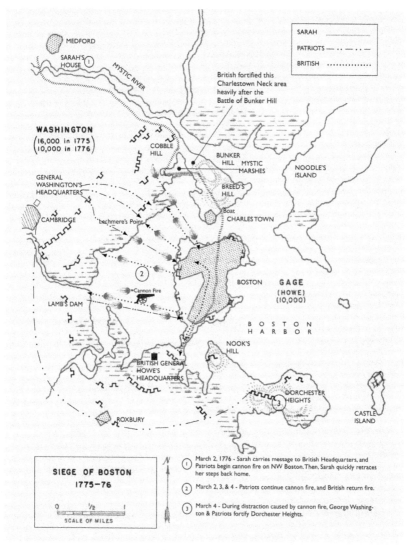

Sarah's secret mission route

She quickly climbed into the boat. Looking up, she said, "Now *that* was Providence!"

Did you know that Providence was a popular term of the time, meaning God's involvement in human events?

Sarah summoned all her strength and rowed across the river to Boston from Charlestown. At this time of year, it usually took two strong men to row across the ice-clogged river. As she reached the shore, she hopped out of the boat and approached the north side of Boston on foot. She saw British sentries posted everywhere. One of them looked in her direction, but she ducked behind a tree. She was familiar with Boston from all the times she and John had visited her brother Nathaniel and his family.

I wish I could visit them right now, she mused, *but I can't do that tonight. I have to keep focused on my assignment to get these papers to General Howe. How in the world am I going to do that?* Just then, a Patriot that she recognized galloped past on a horse. The sentry fired two shots but missed. Watching the horseback rider disappear into the darkness, Sarah had an idea: maybe she could make the papers look like they fell from a Patriot's pouch as he galloped by to deliver messages to fellow Americans trapped in Boston?

While the sentry was looking away, Sarah made a mad dash across the enemy lines and into the city. Memories of happier times came flooding back to her mind. It was familiar ground for her, and she easily found General Howe's tent.

Still staying out of sight, Sarah bent over and ripped open the hem of her skirt to reveal the papers. Then she smashed them into the dirt. She said to herself, "That should make them look like they fell on the ground!"

Spotting a guard standing at the entrance to Howe's tent, Sarah walked confidently toward him. "I must see General Howe. I found some papers on the ground that might be important!" she said.

"Yes, ma'am."

The soldier gestured for her to follow him into the tent. General Howe stood looking over a map spread out on a large wooden table.

"Good evening, madam. What brings you out on this frightfully cold night?"

"Good evening, General Howe. I found these papers on a trail on the north side of the city. I thought you might want to see them because I saw them fall from a Patriot's pouch as he galloped past our sentries."

Howe eyed her with a hint of suspicion. "Thank you, madam, but how do I know that you are loyal to the Crown?"

"I assure you I am a Loyalist, General Howe," Sarah said, in her most convincing manner, as she mimicked a strong British accent, "Why else would I have brought these to you?"

The general didn't respond. He just unfolded the papers, scanned them, and then looked at Sarah with surprise.

"These are official dispatches written in George Washington's own handwriting, with his official signature!" he exclaimed. "This report and map detail his plan of attack. He will be sending troops with cannons to attack from three locations, Lechmere's Point, Cobble Hill, and Lamb's Dam, on the Cambridge side of Boston."

At that exact moment, they heard the loud KABOOM of a cannon from the direction of Cambridge! Both Sarah and General Howe startled.

"I believe you, madam. Thank you for your help!"

Howe ran out of the tent and yelled, "Rally the troops! We are under attack!"

No one noticed Sarah slip away and into the crowd. She smiled to herself. Little did the general know that Cambridge was just a cover-up for General Washington's real plan!

Her heroic mission accomplished, Sarah dashed back to the boat, rowed across the river, and retraced her steps across the Mystic Marshes.

Sarah heads home after successfully completing a deception operation

Finally, just before dawn, Sarah dragged herself across the threshold of her home. "I need sleep!" she said to John as she crawled into bed.

For the next three nights, Sarah and everyone in the Boston area could hear the ear-splitting, continuous, booming bombardment of cannons as the Patriots fired at the British from the 3 locations near Cambridge. The British responded by returning fire on the Americans. But, would the distraction work?

Did you know that General Washington often used deceptive operations like allowing a false battle plan to fall into enemy hands? As in Sarah's story, he sent couriers to plant misleading intelligence; meanwhile, he would put his actual plan in motion. British commanders were distracted by the wrong information and would not realize they were tricked until the battle was over.

George Washington Visits

Medford, March 1776 and October 1789

ifteen days later, Sarah heard a knock at her front door. When she opened it, there stood General Washington himself!

"Please come in, Your Excellency!"

Did you know that George Washington was often referred to by the title "Your Excellency" at that time?

Sarah introduced John and all her children. Sarah was a tiny woman, and by comparison, Washington seemed very tall. He was almost too tall to fit through the doorway. His presence commanded respect, yet he was so friendly, greeting each family member in a kindly manner. He made everyone feel important to him. They sat down to eat refreshments—John's famous rum punch and cookies.

"I wanted to personally thank you, Mrs. Fulton, for carrying the secret message to the British for me. Major Brooks told me about how you tricked General Howe into believing the papers had fallen from a Patriot's pouch. Thanks to the message you delivered, General Howe ordered all his men to the Cambridge side of Boston. As you and all Boston could hear, we fired cannons at them for three nights in a row, but on the third night, we took action. While they were distracted, Brigadier General John Thomas quietly rallied our troops—800 Patriot soldiers and 1,200 workers—and stealthily moved our ammunition to Dorchester Heights. Everything was done and in place early in the morning on March 5."

"That's the sixth anniversary of the Boston Massacre!" exclaimed Sarah.

"Exactly," said Washington. "I was right there alongside them, reminding them of that horrible massacre, which inspired them to move even more speedily to finish by the deadline of the early morning of the fifth."

"I heard that our troops worked feverishly through the night to drag heavy cannons over a wooden structure designed and built by General Rufus Putnam. It's amazing that he created these out of logs and bushels of sticks so that the ammunition could be hauled over the frozen solid ground, to the top of Dorchester."

"Yes, Sarah, and we muffled the sound of our wagon wheels by placing bales of straw on the ground surrounding our fortification maneuvers. We also carried wooden barrels filled with gravel up there to roll down on the enemy if they attempted to recapture the hill the next day. When the British awoke on March 5 to see that Dorchester Heights had been secured and armed, I heard that General Howe was shocked and horrified. He said, 'The rebels have completed more in one night than our troops could have done in one month!'"

Dorchester Heights

"We couldn't have done it without you, Sarah. I appreciate you risking your life so that we could gain the victory. You must remember, though, that your life is still in danger, so for heaven's sake, keep the message you carried and my visit today between us; do not tell anyone about this! The war is not over yet, but now that we have Boston back, your message and our Patriots' work may have just turned the tide of the war. Thank you for saving the day, Sarah!"

"You are welcome, Your Excellency," Sarah responded, blushing, "I did my best, and Providence took care of the rest!"

Did you know that the British planned to counterattack the Patriots later in the day on March 5 and use the British ships in Boston Harbor to reclaim Dorchester Heights? However, Providence was surely involved, as a historically violent storm ravaged Boston later that day. This storm made any counterattack impossible. The British were forced to surrender, and they promised not to burn down the city on their way out if they could be allowed to evacuate by sea without being hurt. The Continental Army agreed, and the British left on March 17.

They headed by sea to Nova Scotia, Canada. Every year on March 17, Bostonians celebrate "Evacuation Day."

Washington turned to go. "My officers are riding into Boston to-day, but I'm off to church. God gave us this victory. I'm going to proclaim a day of thanksgiving and fasting. And then it's on to New York, for I fear the British will attack there next. But I will return someday, and I hope to visit you again."

What a good leader, thought Sarah. His humble actions made it crystal clear that he had no desire to be a king. Some people in his situation would have taken advantage of this victory to ride their horse into Boston and claim all the glory for themselves.

Did you know that Washington would be presented with the first medal ever awarded by the Continental Congress, for this victory in Boston? Although Washington was in a hurry to get to New York before the British attempted to take over the city, he accepted an honorary degree from Harvard University before he left. That was a great honor for a man who had very little formal education. Later, the Declaration of Independence would be signed on July 4, 1776, but the war would not end until September 3, 1783.

Washington was true to his word. On October 29, 1789, he visited Medford again. But this time, he wasn't General Washington; he was President Washington! Just six months before, on April 30, 1789, he had been inaugurated as the first president of the new United States of America.

Sarah Lloyd saw Washington gallop into town on horseback with an entourage of other riders. She ran back home and burst in the door. "Mama, he's here!"

Sarah busied herself with final preparations for his visit. John was busy making his famous rum punch when they heard hoof-beats approaching. The whole family greeted Washington at the door.

"Welcome, Mr. President!" said Sarah. "Please come in."

She invited him to sit in their best chair at the head of the table, where she'd laid out their finest table settings. John ladled his famous hot rum punch out of a silver punch bowl Sarah had purchased for this special occasion.

"You know me well, Mrs. Fulton," said Washington, eyeing the Indian corncakes on a platter nearby. "Those corncakes smell delicious! I hope you have lots of butter and honey too!"

"Yes, I do," said Sarah with a laugh. "I heard that your granddaughter, Nellie, says that your favorite food is corncakes swimming in butter and honey!"

ACTIVITY ~ RECIPES

TRY THESE RECIPES, COURTESY OF MOUNT VERNON LADIES' ASSOCIATION, AND SEE WHICH ONE YOU LIKE BETTER—THE ORIGINAL CORNCAKES THAT GEORGE WASHINGTON ACTUALLY ATE AND LOVED, OR THE MODERN VERSION OF CORNBREAD SERVED AT MOUNT VERNON.

Indian Corncake Recipe

Ingredients

- o 2 cups stone-ground white or yellow cornmeal
- o 1 ½ -2 cups lukewarm water (100-110°F, use a candy thermometer)
- o 1 ¾ ounce package active dry yeast
- o ½ teaspoon salt
- o 1 large egg
- o Mild vegetable oil, for greasing griddle
- o Honey, for serving (optional)
- o Butter, for serving (optional)

Directions

1. The night before you plan to eat the corn cakes, combine 1 cup of the cornmeal, 1 ½ cups of the lukewarm water, and the yeast in a medium-size nonreactive bowl. Whisk well; the mixture will be thin. Cover the bowl tightly and let it sit overnight in a warm place.

2. The next morning, whisk in the remaining 1 cup cornmeal, salt, and one egg. Re-cover the bowl; let it stand 15-20 minutes (allowing the just-added cornmeal to absorb some of the liquid and soften a bit).

3. Check the consistency; it should be close to a thin pancake batter. If you need to, add a little more lukewarm water to achieve this.

4. Heat a cast-iron skillet or griddle over medium-high heat. Oil lightly with a paper towel dipped in oil or nonstick cooking spray.

5. Stir the batter well; using a ladle, pour 3-4 thin, 3-inch pancakes onto the hot skillet. The batter will spread out fairly thin. If it doesn't sizzle a little as you pour it, the skillet isn't hot enough. If it sizzles a lot, you may need to reduce the heat.

6. Now watch closely. Almost immediately, you'll see little bubbles appear throughout. When the top surface is completely dry, and edges are beginning to curl, flip one cake. It should be golden-brown and nicely speckled. Cook the first side about 1 minute and the second side 30-50 seconds. Repeat with remaining cakes and batter, making sure to stir batter occasionally, so it doesn't separate.

7. Serve with honey and butter, if desired.

Cornbread Recipe

Ingredients

- ○ ¾ cup white or yellow cornmeal
- ○ 1 cup flour
- ○ 1/3 cup sugar
- ○ 1 tablespoon baking powder
- ○ ¾ teaspoon salt
- ○ 1 cup milk

- o 1 egg, well beaten
- o 2 tablespoons melted shortening (or butter, margarine, oil)

Directions

1. Preheat oven to 425°F.
2. Sift the dry ingredients into a bowl—cornmeal, flour, sugar, baking powder, and salt.
3. Add milk, egg, and shortening. Mix together.
4. Pour into a greased, shallow 8" x 8" baking dish.
5. Bake for 20 minutes until golden brown.
6. Cut into wedges and serve warm with butter, honey, or jam.

"You know," said Washington between bites, "after I saw you last, I went to New York and formed a spy ring called the Culper Ring. We used your trick, Sarah. One of my spies intentionally dropped some of my dispatch papers with false information so that it looked like it had fallen from a Patriot's pouch. Just like in Boston, this trick distracted the British from the real action that was taking place—French ships arriving in New York Harbor with ammunition and soldiers to aid us in reclaiming New York City."

Did you know that after the Patriots won back New York City in March 1777, George Washington went back to the homes of each of his spies and couriers to thank them for their help? He did the same thing for Sarah.

"Providence was surely with you, as it was with me that night in Boston," said Sarah.

Washington agreed. "Indeed, Providence has been with us in the founding of our new nation."

Chapter 10

A VISIT FROM LAFAYETTE AND A LONG LIFE

Medford, 1790-1835

*I*t was well known that Sarah's humble home was always hospitably open to her family, especially to her brother Nathaniel's children, as well as to her many friends. It was said that the latch string was always out on her front door so that people could pull on it and open the door to visit her. (Most people kept their latch string inside the door so they could keep unwelcome visitors out.) Many people said that Sarah was never afraid of man or beast. She once told her grandson, "I never turned my back on anything." She had a tradition of walking a long distance to the Unitarian Church every Sunday, even when she became really old. Sadly, Sarah's husband John had become sick and died on February 9th, 1790, leaving her a widow at the age of forty-nine. His death certificate listed "complications puking" as his cause of death.

Despite losing her husband, Sarah was able to support herself by taking care of local sick and elderly people.

Many years after the American Revolution and George Washington's visit, she would entertain another special guest, General Lafayette. He was a French military officer who had fought for the

Patriots during the war, and he was a good friend of Washington and Major Brooks.

General Lafayette had been invited, in 1824, to be an honored guest of the American people for a year. When his ship arrived in New York Harbor, tens of thousands of people were waiting to greet him with cheers, clapping, and loud singing of French songs. He was whisked away in a fine carriage drawn by four white horses to be the star of a parade through New York City. For two hours, the crowd threw confetti and flowers in celebration of his arrival.

Lafayette then went on a whirlwind tour of America, visiting with all the important dignitaries of the day, including President James Monroe and Major John Brooks. He was also invited to countless ceremonies, churches, and social events such as dances and formal dinners at every place he stopped. He was extremely popular with all the American people for being a Revolutionary War hero.

One of the formal dinners in his honor was held at the Royall House in Medford, Massachusetts. This elaborate dinner boasted the finest menu. All the townspeople contributed their best tablecloths, china, silver, and glassware for the occasion. Only men were invited to this event. Yet, Lafayette made time before dinner to visit eighty-four-year-old Sarah Bradlee Fulton.

That evening, Sarah set out her finest china and served General Lafayette rum punch from the same silver punch bowl that had served George Washington many years before.

"I'm sorry that my husband, John, couldn't be here. He passed away in 1790. I wish he was here."

"Indeed, that must have been such a loss for you," said General Lafayette, taking a sip of his rum punch.

George Washington had passed on December 14, 1799, of a respiratory illness complicated by a treatment of blood-letting that was popular at the time. His passing had been a sad and difficult time for Sarah and everyone, but especially for Lafayette. She spoke to him gently, "You must miss President Washington."

"Yes, Mrs. Fulton, I miss him like he was my own father. We met when I was a young man in America, and he was like an adopted father to me. I appreciated many things about him, especially his fatherly kindness towards me and his kindness to all kinds of people. Even though he was an important general and later, president, he had a noble and friendly way of greeting officers and citizens alike."

"Yes, sir, I remember that about him, too. I'm sorry for your loss because he loved you like a son."

Tears welled up in their eyes as they remembered their beloved leader, Washington.

Lafayette leaned back in his chair. "It's good to remember with you, Mrs. Fulton. Thank you for all the heroic things you did during the Revolutionary War. You were so brave and different—in a good way. Most women wouldn't have done such daring and bold things."

"Thank you, General."

Lafayette stayed as long as he could, considering his heavy social schedule. As his visit with Sarah came to an end, he brought out a beautiful, ruby-red garnet pin surrounded by tiny pearls in a gold setting and humbly presented it to Sarah as a gift. It represented his appreciation for her brave actions as a true founding mother, a Patriot of the American Revolution, and a secret courier for George Washington.

Sarah lived a long and happy life. On the morning of November 9, 1835, her grown daughters found that she had died in her sleep, with a peaceful smile on her face. Sarah would have been ninety-five years old the following month. She was buried in the old Salem Street Cemetery, and the stone which marks her grave was taken from the doorstep of her house. The street she lived on was renamed Fulton Street in her honor.

Did you know that people didn't usually live as long as Sarah did at that time? The average life span was 38.

The inscription on her grave marker is as follows:

SARAH BRADLEE FULTON

1740-1835

A HEROINE OF THE REVOLUTION

ERECTED BY THE

SARAH BRADLEE FULTON CHAPTER

D.A.R.

1900

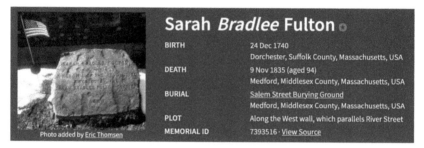

https://www.findagrave.com/memorial/7393516/sarah-fulton

Grandma was at the end of Sarah's story. "Ellen, Sarah lived her life with no fear, and at times she was a bit rough around the edges. But it was her boldness that made her a heroine and allowed her to play an important role in the American Revolution."

Grandma leans back in her chair and turns to look at me. "And *that* is the story of Sarah Bradlee Fulton and how she got the Lafayette pin."

"Wow! What a great story, Grandma. Somebody should write a book about that!"

EPILOGUE

Now it's time for you to take action! I hope that Sarah's story will inspire you to help make America and the world a better place. Even little things make a difference. For example, you can organize a fundraiser for a cause that you care about, take food to an elderly neighbor, pick up trash in your neighborhood, or take charge of recycling in your home.

Be yourself and use your talents to contribute to your community. George Washington and the founding men and women of the United States had high hopes for our democracy. Within God's Providence, you were born for such a time as this. Don't be afraid to be the special person that you were created to be. Let your light shine!

~ Ellen Chervenick

ACKNOWLEDGMENTS

First of all, I would like to thank God for His providence in my life and for helping me through my own Mystic Marshes.

To my husband, Joe, thank you for your encouragement. Your question, "When are you going to finish your book?" helped push me to completion. Thank you for all of your help in many practical ways including tech-support.

I am indebted to Dr. Patrice Stark for her research and input about genealogy.

Thank you, Margaret G., Kim MacDonald, Denise Wey, Sheryl Cobb, Jacki Warych, and Dr. Jeff Conklin for offering insightful feedback.

To my crafty cohorts, Kelsea, Meredith, and Melanie, I love our art group and appreciate you lending an ear to my story.

Thanks to Colleen Green for cooking the corncakes and cornbread in your test kitchen.

Also, a special shout out to my cousins: Linda, Herb, Daryl, Lauren, George, Sid, and Nate. I'm glad we're family.

Danelle Young, thank you for helping me format and add finishing touches to *Sarah Saves the Day*. I appreciate your attention to detail.

Thank you, Ali Dent, for the beautiful cover design and all of the heart-felt and creative expertise that you have contributed to publishing this book. I could not have done this without you!

ABOUT THE AUTHOR

Ellen Chervenick is an artist and the author and illustrator of *Sarah Saves the Day*. She holds a master's degree in TESOL (Teaching English to Speakers of Other Languages) from Biola University and has taught art, ESL, and special education. Ellen's graduate school research (on using sensory activities to teach) inspired this educational book. She once taught a group of fifth graders about the Revolutionary War by impersonating her ancestor Sarah Bradlee Fulton and providing sensory activities. It's one of her favorite teaching memories. Ellen lives on a small ranch in northern California with her husband Joe, daughter Savannah, and their menagerie of pets.

ADDENDUM

Several records confirm the authenticity of Sarah's life events. Lucretia Butler Fulton was the ninth and last surviving child of Sarah (Bradlee) Fulton. Per research by Dr. Patrice Stark, Lucretia died in 1872 at Cambridge, MA and is the source of the Fulton artifacts and family folklore. The first account Dr. Stark found describing this Fulton Family was published in 1873, shortly after Lucretia's death.

Eliza Gill wrote about General Lafayette's visit to Medford in the Medford Historical Society Papers Vol. 15 (published in 1912, with newspaper excerpts from November 1824), "He [Lafayette] called on our Revolutionary heroine, Mrs. John Fulton (born Sarah Bradlee). At this time, he presented her with a breast-pin, now in possession of descendants of hers (Rindge family) in Cambridge."

Helen Tilden Wild, another descendant, wrote an account of Sarah's story for the *Medford Register* in August of 1898. Most other references to Sarah are derived from Helen's article.

Edward Rowe Snow authenticates Sarah's involvement in the Boston Tea Party in his book *Tales of Sea and Shore*.

Adam Zeilinski, who wrote "Sir William Howe: The Man Who Could Not Quell a Rebellion," in *Revolutionary War History, American Battlefield Trust*, supports the notion that deceptive information was given to Sir William. "By March, Howe had reports of the American positions adjacent to Boston. Plans were being made to send two amphibious assaults on their position. At the same time, on the night of March 4, Washington directed his men to build fortifications on Dorchester Heights, the highest point in Boston Harbor."

The seven-year-old girl who stitched the sampler pictured in chapter two (Ellen Antoinette Smith) is my great-great-grandmother. Her daughters, Nellie and Clara, both married descendants of Sarah and John Fulton's children.

BIBLIOGRAPHY

Albus, Brenda Ely. *A Woman Fearing Nothing: The Story of Sarah Bradlee Fulton, A Revolutionary War Heroine.* Self-published, Lulu.com, 2015.

"Boston Massacre." Wikipedia. Accessed February 10, 2020. https://en.wikipedia.org/wiki/Boston_Massacre.

Brooks, Charles. *History of Medford.* Published by James M. Usher in the Register of Families Genealogical Section of the New York Public Library, 1855. Page 514.

Brumwell, Stephen. *George Washington, Gentleman Warrior.* Quercus, 2012.

Chervenick, Ellen. *Schema Theory: Teaching U.S. History to Beginning Amnesty Students.* Master's Thesis. William Carey International University, 1992.

Doggett, Samuel Bradlee. *History of the Bradlee Family.* Boston, MA: Press of Rockwell and Churchill, 1878.

Forrest, Kim. "The (Surprising!) History of the White Wedding Dress." *Wedding Wire,* March 12, 2019. https://www.weddingwire.com/wedding-ideas/white-wedding-dress-history.

Gill, Eliza M. "Lafayette's Visit to Medford. People and Incidents Relating Thereto Reviewed." *Medford Historical Society Papers* Vol. 15 (1912, with newspaper excerpts from November 1824).

Hands, Herbert Rindge. Letter to the family, written August 13, 1968.

Hands, Madeleine Rindge. Personal interview with the author, 1964.

"Intelligence in the War of Independence." *Central Intelligence Agency website.* Last modified September 6, 2017. https://www.cia.gov/library/publications/intelligence-history/intelligence.

Kilmeade, Brian, and Don Yaeger. *George Washington's Secret Six: The Spy Ring That Saved the American Revolution.* New York: Sentinel, 2014.

Labaree, Benjamin Woods. *The Boston Tea Party.* Boston: Northwestern University Press, 1979.

Nelson, Ken. "Colonial America for Kids: Food and Cooking." *Ducksters Education Site.* ducksters.com, 2020.

Perry, Leonard. "Liberty Tea." *University of Vermont.* Accessed March 2020. https://pss.uvm.edu/ppp/articles/liberty.html.

Ponder, Jon. "Sorry Teabaggers, Washington and Franklin Opposed the Boston Tea Party." *Pensito Review.* Accessed March 2020. http://www.pensitoreview.com/2011/06/08/sorry-tea-baggers-washington-and-franklin-opposed-the-boston-tea-party/.

Saint-Bris, Gonzague. *Lafayette, Hero of the American Revolution.* New York: Pegasus Books, 2010.

Snow, Edward Rowe. *Tales of Sea and Shore.* New York: Dodd, Mead, and Company, 1966.

Stark, Dr. Patrice. Phone and email communications with the author for genealogy research, 2012–2015.

"The Boston Tea Party Song," *Jam Campus*, (Parody of Pharrell Williams- "Happy"), YouTube, October 5, 2015.

Whelan, Frank. "In the America of 1787, big families are the norm and life expectancy is 38", *The Morning Call*, June 28, 1987.

Wild, Helen Tilden. "Sarah Bradlee Fulton", *Medford Register*. August 1898.

Zielinski, Adam E., "Sir William Howe: The Man Who Could Not Quell a Rebellion", *Revolutionary War History, American Battlefield Trust*, battlefields.org

CPSIA information can be obtained
at www.ICGtesting.com
Printed in the USA
BVHW051448220321
603180BV00012B/1651